Toddlers' Action Bible

Toddlers' Action
Bible

Robin Currie
Illustrated by Bill Clark

SAINT LOUIS

For Jeff Santee, who always believed

Scripture quotations taken from the HOLY BIBLE, NEW INTERNATIONAL VERSION®. NIV®. Copyright © 1973, 1978, 1984 by International Bible Society. Used by permission of Zondervan Publishing House. All rights reserved.

Copyright © 1998 Concordia Publishing House
3558 S. Jefferson Avenue, St. Louis, MO 63118-3968
Manufactured in the United States of America

Library of Congress Cataloging-in-Publication Data

Currie, Robin, 1948-
    Toddlers' action Bible / Robin Currie.
        p.   cm.
    Summary: A collection of twenty Old and New Testament stories told with interactive devotions for the parent or teacher to act out with children.
    ISBN 0-570-05030-8
    1. Bible stories, English. [1. Bible stories.] I. Title.
BS551.2.C88   1998
220.9′505—dc21
                                                     97-24651
                                                 AC

2   3   4   5   6   7   8   9   10   07   06   05   04   03   02   01   00   99   98

Contents

It Is Good!

God Creates the World *(Genesis 1:1–2:3)*

Dark, dark, dark.
Close eyes. Can you see anything at all?
God was there in the darkness, getting ready to make the world. First, God made light.
Open eyes.
God said, "It is good."
Nod head yes.
There was water everywhere. God put some of the water in the sky.
Point up.
God took the water on the earth and put it in rivers and oceans.
Wiggle fingers to make waves.
That left places for dry land. God made flat places …
Hold palms out.
And pointy mountains.
Touch fingertips together to make a mountain.
God said, "It is good."
Nod and say "good" together.
God made cherry trees and pine trees.
Reach up high to touch branches on a tree.

God made grapes and bananas.

Do you like bananas?
"Yum!"

God said, "It is good."

Nod and say "good!"

God made the plants with seeds.

Can you curl up like a tiny seed?

God made the shining sun to help the plants grow.

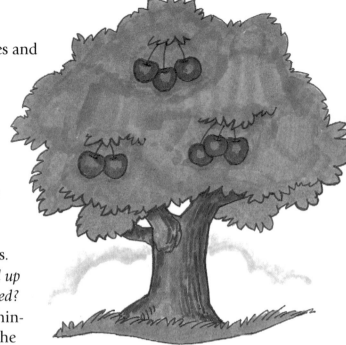

Touch fingertips overhead to make the sun.

God put the moon in the nighttime sky.

Rest cheek on hands as if asleep.

God made twinkling little stars.

Wiggle your fingers in the air.

God said, "It is good."

Nod and say "good!"

God made sparrows and crows to fly in the sky.

Flap arms.

God made goldfish and sharks to swim in the water.

Move arms in a swimming motion.

God said, "It is good!"

Nod and say "good!"

God made big elephants and walruses.

How big is an elephant?

God made soft bunnies and furry kittens.

Pat cheek.

God made prickly porcupines and the duck-billed platypus.

Gently poke each other.

God said, "It is good!"

Nod and say "good!"

God wanted someone to wake up in the morning ...

Yawn.

And say "good morning" to Him.

"Good morning, God!"

So God made people. God made just two people at first.

Hold up two fingers.

Their names were Adam and Eve. God knew there would be more. God said, "It is good!"

Nod and say "good!"

God said to the people, "Take care of My wonderful world."

Rock arms in caring, cradling motion.

Then God said, "It is good!"

Nod and say "good!"

Dear God, thank You for mountains and stars and soft bunnies. Thank You for making me too! In Jesus' name. Amen.

✷ Remember the Story of Creation ✷

Go to the window and point to things that are part of God's creation. Look up in the sky, at the trees and the plants, at the people walking by. Help your child draw a "Thank You, God" picture.

Will It Ever Stop Raining?

Noah Builds an Ark *(Genesis 6:1–9:17)*

Noah pounded with a big, big hammer.
> *Make hammering motion.* "Bam! Bam! Bam!"
God said, "Noah, build a big ark."
> *Spread arms wide.*

"Make it big enough for your family and two of every animal."
Hold up two fingers.
Noah did not live by a lake or a river. Why did he need an ark?
Shrug.
God said, "I am going to make it rain and rain. Soon there will be no dry land at all. You will be safe in the ark."
Reach up and wiggle fingers down to make rain.
So Noah built an ark.
"Bam! Bam! Bam!"
Then Noah loaded food for all the animals. It was a big job!
Wipe forehead. "Whew!"
Then Noah started loading the animals—two by two.
Hold up two fingers.
First came fast animals like the cheetahs.
Move hand in zooming motion. "Zoom!"
Then came big animals like polar bears.
How big were the polar bears?
Friendly animals like dogs came.
What animal would you like for a pet?
Tiny animals like ladybugs came.
Walk fingers up arm like a ladybug crawling.
And last came very slow animals like turtles.
Walk fingers very slowly.
When all the animals were safe inside, God sent the rain.
Wiggle fingers for rain. "Pitter, patter. Pitter, patter."

Noah and his family and the animals cuddled close together.

"Quick! Give me a hug."

It rained for a long, long time.

Wiggle fingers. "Pitter, patter. Pitter, patter."

Then God made the rain stop.

Shhhh!

The sun came out.

Touch fingertips overhead.

Noah waited for the earth to dry. Then Noah and the animals came out.

What do you think the animals did?

The fast animals and big animals and tiny animals and friendly animals and even the slow animals ran out of the ark.

How fast can you run?

They ate the grass and rolled on hills covered with flowers. God had kept them safe!

"Hooray!"

God said to Noah, "Never again will I send so much rain to cover the earth. I will keep My promise." God put a colorful rainbow in the sky.

Trace rainbow arch in air.

God kept Noah safe. He keeps you safe too.

Hug.

Dear God, thank You for always keeping me safe. In Jesus' name. Amen.

✷ Remember the Story of Noah's Ark ✷

Help your child gather stuffed animals. Make an ark out of a box or throw a blanket over some chairs and crawl in. Help your child draw a rainbow to hang over your ark.

Count the Stars in the Sky

God's Promises to Abraham and Sarah *(Genesis 12:1–21:5)*

Abraham and Sarah had lots of goats and sheep.
   "Baa, baa. Baa, baa."
Abraham and Sarah lived in a tent.
   Touch fingertips together to make a tent.
One day God said, "Abraham, I will give you a new land."
   Nod head yes.
God said, "Look up in the sky. Can you count all the stars?"
   Point up. Pretend to count stars.

"There will be more people in your family than all the stars in the sky."

Point to all the stars.

"One of the babies will be My own Son, Jesus. He will show My love to everyone."

Clasp hands over heart.

Abraham and Sarah walked to their new land.

Pat hands on knees.

They walked and walked.

Pat hands on knees.

The sheep and goats walked and walked.

Pat hands on knees. "Baa. Baa."

Finally they came to their new home. There was green grass and plenty of water. God had brought Abraham and Sarah to a good place.

Smile.

But Abraham and Sarah did not have a child.

Shake head no.

Abraham and Sarah were very old. How could they have a baby?

Hold palms out and shrug.

But God can do anything.

Nod head yes.

God gave Abraham and Sarah a son. They named their baby Isaac. He made his mother and father so happy.

Happily cradle baby in arms and rock.

God kept all His promises to Abraham. God keeps all His promises to you.

Dear God, thank You for giving me all that I need. Thank You for sending Jesus for me. Amen.

✯ Remember the Story of Abraham, Sarah, and Isaac ✯

Look at your child's baby pictures. Tell your child how happy you were to have a baby—just as Abraham and Sarah were happy to have Isaac. Together list all the things your child can do now that a baby can't do.

All 12 Brothers

Joseph and His Brothers *(Genesis 37:1–47:12)*

What a big family Jacob had. He had 12 sons!
  Count to 12.
Jacob gave his son Joseph a beautiful new coat.
  What color is your coat?

Joseph put on the coat and showed his brothers. They were angry.

Make an angry face.

They sent Joseph away to Egypt.

Point finger and say, "Go away!"

Joseph had never been to Egypt, but he knew God would take care of him.

Hug yourself.

God helped Joseph become an important man in Egypt. Joseph made sure everyone had enough food to eat.

What do you like to eat?

Back at Jacob's home there was not enough food for all 11 brothers and their families.

Count to 11.

Everyone was hungry.

Rub tummy.

Jacob heard that there was plenty of food in Egypt. He sent the brothers to Egypt. They did not know they would be asking Joseph for food!

Hold palms out and shrug. "What will Joseph do?"

The brothers went to Egypt and asked for food.

Cup hands and hold them out as if begging.

Joseph said, "Look! I am your brother."
Point to self.

The brothers remembered how mean they had been to Joseph. They were afraid.

Hug self and shiver.

But Joseph said, "I forgive you. Take all the food you need."

Spread arms wide.

Joseph said, "Bring my father to Egypt so we can live as a family again."

Cheer: "Hooray for Joseph!"

....

Dear God, help me forgive others. Help me share with my family and friends. In Jesus' name. Amen.

✵ Remember the Story of Joseph and His Brothers ✵

Let your child help bake some cookies or spread peanut butter on crackers. Invite family members or friends to share with you.

What's in the Basket?

God Saves Baby Moses *(Exodus 1:1–2:10)*

Shhhh!

Hold finger to lips. "Shhhh!"

Mother wanted her baby to be very quiet.

Cradle arms and rock baby.

If the soldiers heard him cry, they would take him from her.

Hold finger to lips. "Shhhh!"

The king of Egypt was mean to God's people. He made them work hard.

Wipe brow. "Whew!"

The king wanted to take all the boy babies away from their mothers. The mothers cried.

Hide face and pretend to cry.

The baby's mother made a basket and sealed it so it could float.

Do your toys float in the bathtub?

Then she put in soft blankets.

Pat cheek.

She put her baby in the basket.

Hold finger to lips. "Shhhh!"

Mother put the basket in the river. She asked God to keep her baby safe.

Fold hands.

The baby liked the gentle rocking of the water.

Rock back and forth. "Whee!"

The baby's sister, Miriam, watched the basket float on the river.

Shade eyes with hand.

A princess came to take a bath in the river. She saw the basket.

Point in surprise.

Miriam thought, Oh no, what if the mean king finds my brother?

Clap hands to cheeks. "Oh no!"

The princess picked up the baby and smiled.

Cradle arms and smile.

She said, "A baby boy! I will call him 'Moses.' He will be a prince of Egypt."

Smile and rock baby.

Miriam ran to get her mother.
Pat hands on knees.
"Mother, the princess will take care of baby Moses. He will be safe."
Cheer: "Hooray!"
Mother smiled and said, "Thank You, God. Thank You for taking care of baby Moses."
Fold hands.

....

Dear God, thank You for keeping me safe all the time. In Jesus' name. Amen.

✯ Remember the Story of Baby Moses ✯

Fill the sink, tub, or a swimming pool with water and float plastic containers. Give small toys a ride in the containers just as Moses rode in his basket boat.

A Path through the Water

God Parts the Red Sea *(Exodus 12:1–17:7)*

Moses grew up.
Reach hand up high.
God told Moses to lead His people to a new home.
Point away from you.
Moses went to Egypt's king. He said, "Let God's people go."

Point away from you.
But the king said, "No!"
Stamp foot. Shake head. "No!"
Moses asked again. He said, "Let God's people go."
Point away from you.
But the king said, "No!"
Stamp foot. Shake head. "No!"
God sent troubles to the king's people. Finally the king said, "Go!"
Point away from you.

Moses told God's people, "Get ready. Go."

Point away from you.

God's people set out to walk to the Promised Land.

Pat hands on knees.

The children walked.

Pat hands on knees.

The donkeys and sheep and goats walked.

Pat hands on knees.

The happy people sang as they walked.

Sing a favorite song together as you pat hands on knees.

The people walked until they came to some water
called the Red Sea. What should they do?

*Scratch head,
look puzzled.*

Clop, clop,
clop-clop!

*Loudly pat
hands on
knees.
"Clop,
clop,
clop-
clop!"*

28

Horses were coming! Clop, clop, clop-clop!

Loudly pat hands on knees. "Clop, clop, clop-clop!"

The king's soldiers were coming to take the people back to Egypt!

Hug self and shiver. "No!"

God told Moses what to do. "Hold your walking stick over the water."

Hold one arm out straight.

The water parted and made a dry path for the people to walk on.

Cheer: "Hooray!"

The people hurried across the path.

Quickly pat hands on knees.

The children hurried across the path.

Quickly pat hands on knees.

The donkeys and sheep and goats hurried across the path.

Quickly pat hands on knees.

Moses put his walking stick down.

Raise, then lower, arm.

God made the water come rushing back together!

Clap hands together, "Whoosh!"

The king's soldiers could not catch God's people.

Cheer: "Hooray!"

God kept His people safe. He led them to their new home.

Clap hands for joy.

Dear God, keep my family safe when we go places.
I'm glad You are with me all the time. In Jesus' name.
Amen.

✯ Remember the Story of the Exodus ✯

At bath time remember all the water Moses faced at
the Red Sea. Talk about all the places that you and
your child go where God is with you. That's everywhere!

The Brave Shepherd

David and Goliath *(1 Samuel 16:1–17:51)*

The sheep finished drinking water.
  "Baa! Baa!"
David, the shepherd boy, led the sheep to some good grass to eat.
  "Baa, baa. Baa, baa."
David sat down to watch the sheep. He sang a song to them.
  Sing a favorite song together.

A messenger ran up to David. His father needed him. David ran home.

Quickly pat hands on knees.

David's father said, "Your brothers are fighting in the army. Take this food to them. Find out how they are."

Pat hands on knees.

David's brothers were sad.

Make a sad face.

They said, "Every day a big, big soldier named Goliath says, 'Fight me!' "

Hold fist up high.

"No one is brave enough to fight him," the brothers said sadly.

Shake head sadly.

David said, "God helps me fight lions."

Roar like a lion.

"God helps me fight bears."

Growl like a bear.

"God will help me fight a giant soldier too."

Place hand bravely over heart.

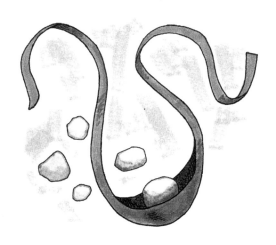

David took his sling and five smooth stones.

Count to five.

Goliath laughed. "They are sending a boy to do a man's job!"

Laugh loudly like Goliath.

David asked God to help him.

Fold hands.

David put a stone in his sling and waved it over his head.

Pretend to wave sling overhead. "Swish!"

Plunk! The stone hit Goliath!

Tap forehead. "Plunk!"

Plop! Goliath fell on the ground.

Clap one hand on the other to show Goliath falling.

The soldiers cheered, "Hooray for David!"

Cheer: "Hooray for David!"

....

Dear God, thank You for being with me always, even when I am afraid. In Jesus' name. Amen.

✯ Remember the Story of David and Goliath ✯

Build a pen with blocks and put in a lot of cotton-ball sheep. Sing a song to the sheep together. Build a tall stack of blocks and call it Goliath. Let your child knock it down.

Lions Are Big Kitty Cats

God Protects Daniel in the Lions' Den *(Daniel 6:1–28)*

Daniel prayed to God every day.
Fold hands.
The king liked Daniel.
Nod head fondly.
That made the king's friends angry. "Let's get Daniel in trouble," they said.
Shake fist and make an angry face.
"Make a new law," the friends told the king. "Say that everyone should pray to you!"
Fold hands.
"If someone doesn't pray to you, throw him to the lions!"
"Roar!"
The king liked the new law.
Nod happily.
Daniel did not.
Shake head no.
Daniel said, "I like to help the king. But I only pray to God."
Fold hands.
"Daniel is praying to God!" the friends said. "Throw him to the lions!"
"Roar!"

The king did not want to hurt Daniel, but he had made the law. He threw Daniel into a pen with lions.

"Roar!"

The king was worried. He got up early in the morning.

Yawn and stretch.

He went to the pen. Why weren't the lions roaring?

Cup hand to ear.

"Daniel, are you all right?" the king called.

Lean forward and call with hand cupped around mouth.

"I am fine," Daniel said. "God sent an angel to close the lions' mouths."

Clap hand over mouth.

The king was delighted.

Clap hands.

Daniel said, "I knew God would not let the lions hurt me. I like to help you, but I will only pray to God."

Fold hands.

"Daniel's God is the true God," said the king. "We will all pray to Him."
Fold hands.

Dear God, I know You will keep me safe. I'm glad I can pray to You anytime. In Jesus' name. Amen.

✻ Remember the Story of Daniel in the Lions' Den ✻

Together, draw pictures of things your child fears—storms, big dogs, the dark, etc. Then draw the international symbol for no (a circle with a slash through it) across your pictures.

Pray with your child, thanking God for always keeping you safe.

What's All the Singing About?

The Birth of Jesus *(Luke 2:1–20)*

Shhhh!
Hold finger to lips. "Shhhh!"

Everyone was asleep in Bethlehem.

Rest cheek on hands.

The cats were sleeping. The doves were sleeping.

Rest cheek on hands.

Even the old gray donkey was sleeping.

Rest cheek on hands.

Joseph and Mary walked slowly into Bethlehem.

Slowly pat hands on knees.

In Bethlehem, there was no place to stay.

Shake head no.

Joseph and Mary walked to a stable.

Slowly pat hands on knees.

They could sleep in the stable.

Rest cheek on hands.

A cow peeked at them.

"Mooo!"

Little mice scurried under the hay.

"Squeak!"

A tired little donkey fell asleep.

Hold finger to lips. "Shhhh!"

Joseph and Mary fell asleep.

Hold finger to lips. "Shhhh!"

In the middle of the night, the old gray donkey woke up.

"Hee-haw!"

The cow woke up.

"*Mooo!*"

The mice woke up.

"*Squeak!*"

The animals heard a new sound.

"*Waa! Waa, waa!*"

Mary held a brand-new baby in her arms.

Cradle arms and rock baby.

Shhhh! The baby wants to sleep.

Hold finger to lips. "Shhhh!"

Near Bethlehem shepherds fell asleep in the fields with their sheep.

Rest cheek on hands.

They heard a loud noise!

Open eyes wide.

Up in the sky was an angel!

Point to sky.

The sky was bright with light.

Put hands over eyes.

The angel said, "Don't be afraid. I have good news. Today in Bethlehem your Savior has been born. You will find a baby wrapped in cloths and lying in a manger."

Cradle baby in arms.

Then the sky was full of angels singing a wonderful song
about God's peace.

What do you think the angels' song sounded like?

Just like that, the angels were gone.

Clap hands.

The shepherds ran to Bethlehem.

Quickly pat hands on knees.

They looked in big houses, but Jesus wasn't there.

Shake head no.

They looked in fancy houses, but Jesus wasn't there.

Shake head no.

They looked in important houses, but Jesus wasn't there.

Where do you think Jesus was?

The shepherds looked in a little stable, and they found Jesus.

Point to Jesus in the picture.

Mary let the shepherds look at Jesus. He was wrapped in cloths and sleeping in a manger.

Rest cheek on hands.

The shepherds were quiet.

Shhhh!

But after they left the barn, the shepherds were not quiet at all!

"Hooray! Jesus is born!"

The cats woke up.

"Meow!"

The doves woke up!

"Coo!"

The shepherds told everyone, "We have seen our Savior! His name is Jesus. The angels told us about Him."

Who can you tell about Jesus?

Dear God, thank You for sending Jesus into the world as a little baby. I know He understands everything about me because He was a little child too. Amen.

✳ Remember the Story of Jesus' Birth ✳

Unpack your nativity set—even if it's the middle of summer— or buy a simple plastic one for your child to enjoy. Let your child move the figures as you tell the story together. Remind your child often that Jesus loves him or her.

Follow That Star!

The Visit of the Wise Men *(Matthew 2:1–12)*

Mary and Joseph knew Jesus was a special child. They took good care of Him.

Rock the baby.

The shepherds knew Jesus was a special baby.

Nod head yes.

They told people in Bethlehem Jesus was their Savior.

Nod head yes.

Most other people didn't know anything at all about Jesus.

Shake head no.

Far away, Wise Men saw a special star in the sky.

Point to sky.

They knew the star meant a new king was born, but they didn't know where to find Him.

Raise palms in a questioning gesture.

They packed all their books and clothes on camels.

What do you pack to go on a trip?

The Wise Men took three presents for the new king.

Count to three.

They road their camels in the direction of the star.

Camels go (pat hands on knees and sway) "galoom-pa, galoompa" when they walk.

Sometimes they rode over hot desert sand.

Wipe brow. "Whew!"

Sometimes they rode over cold mountains.

Shiver.

Finally the Wise Men came to the big city of Jerusalem.

Spread arms wide.

They asked to see the new king. But there was no new king in Jerusalem.

Shake head no.

They asked King Herod where they could find the baby king. But he did not know.

Shake head no.

Teachers who knew God's Word said, "The baby was born in Bethlehem."

Hold hands together to form a Bible.

The Wise Men rode their camels very fast to Bethlehem.

Quickly pat hands on knees and sway back and forth.
"Galoompa, galoompa, galoompa, galoompa."

They followed the star right to the house where Jesus was.

Point to Jesus in the picture.

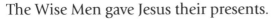

The Wise Men gave Jesus their presents.

> *Count to three.*

That night God talked to the Wise Men in a dream.

> *Rest cheek on hands.*

"King Herod wants to hurt the baby. Don't go back to Jerusalem."

> "*Shhhh. Don't tell anyone.*"

So the Wise Men got back on their camels and rode home another way.

> *Pat hands on knees and sway.* "*Galoompa, galoompa, galoompa.*"

They were so happy that they had found the new King.

> *Smile really big.*

....

Dear God, thank You for giving me the gift of Jesus. Help me to share the Good News about Him with others. Amen.

✶ Remember the Story of the Wise Men ✶

Imagine together that you are traveling on camels. How would it feel? Where would you go on a camel? Who would you see there? Donate canned goods to a food pantry as a "present" to Jesus from your family.

The Teachers Were Amazed

The Boy Jesus Visits the Temple *(Luke 2:41–52)*

Mary took good care of little Jesus.
Cradle arms and rock baby.
He learned to walk and talk and feed Himself.
Do you remember when you learned to walk?
Maybe Jesus liked to play with little lambs.
"Baa! Baa!"
Maybe He fed a little donkey a carrot.
"Hee-haw! Hee-haw!"
As He grew a little bigger, Jesus probably helped Mary carry water from the well.
Where do we get our water?
Maybe He played tag and follow-the-leader with His friends.
What do you like to play with your friends?
When Jesus was older, He learned to read God's Word.
Pretend to read this book.
He even helped Joseph in the carpenter shop. He could pick up nails and sweep the sawdust away.
Sweep, sweep, sweep with a broom.

One exciting day Mary packed food for a long trip. Joseph did not go to the carpenter shop.

Clap hands in excitement.

Mary and Joseph told Jesus they were taking Him to Jerusalem. There He would see the wonderful marketplace full of good food.

What is your favorite food?

He would see the big wall around Jerusalem.

Trace a wall around Jerusalem with your finger.

And He would see the temple—the church where people worshiped God.

What is the name of our church?

At last they came to Jerusalem.

Pat hands on knees.

The wall around the city was big, and there were people everywhere. Maybe Mary bought oranges and dates and a new water jug.

What do we buy at the store?

Maybe Joseph talked to other carpenters about making chairs and doors.

Hammer fist on palm.

But Jesus liked listening to the teachers in the temple who read God's Word.

Point to ears.

The days went quickly. Soon it was time to go home.

Where do we look to see what time it is?

Joseph and Mary started the long walk home. They walked through tall grass.

Rub hands together. "Swish-swish."

They waded across a little stream.

Tap hands on knees. "Splish, splash. Splish, splash."

When it started to get dark, Mary wondered, Where is Jesus?

Where do you think He was?

Mary and Joseph ran back to Jerusalem to find Jesus.

Quickly pat hands on knees.

They ran back through the little stream.

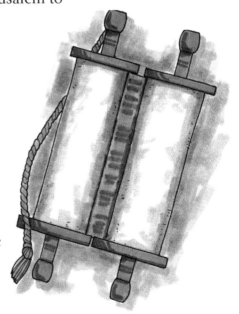

Tap hands on knees. "Splish, splash. Splish, splash."

They ran back through the tall grass.

Rub hands together. "Swish-swish."

They ran through the gate in the tall wall.

Quickly pat hands on knees.

Mary and Joseph looked in the marketplace. Where was Jesus?

Cup hand over eyes.

They looked and looked for three days.

Count to three.

Finally they looked in the big temple.

Join fingertips overhead.

And there was Jesus.

Wipe brow. "Whew!"

Jesus was listening ...

Point to ears.

And talking.

Point to mouth.

The teachers were amazed at how well Jesus knew God's Word.

Clasp hand to cheek and gasp in amazement.

Mary said, "We were worried about You, Jesus. Why didn't You come with us?"

Shake finger as if scolding.

Jesus said, "I need to do the work of God, My Father."
Point to heaven.
Mary and Joseph and Jesus walked home to Nazareth.
Slowly pat hands on knees.
There Jesus continued to grow a little each day, just like you.
Raise hand in stair steps.
Finally He was all grown up.
How tall will you be when you're grown up?

....

Dear God, I like to learn about You and talk about You too. Thank You for helping me grow—just like Jesus. Amen.

☆ Remember the Story of Jesus in the Temple ☆

When you take your child to church, point out the different areas of the worship space—the altar, the lectern, the pulpit, the baptismal font, the choir loft, etc. Talk about what happens during the service—reading God's Word, listening to the sermon, praying and singing, taking communion, praying during a Baptism. Look closely at the stained-glass windows and discuss any imagery your child asks about.

Be Still!

Jesus Calms the Storm *(Mark 4:35–41)*

When Jesus grew up, He told everyone about God's love.
> *Point to Jesus in the picture.*

Jesus asked 12 men to be His special helpers called disciples.
> *Count to 12.*

The disciples stayed close to Jesus and learned all about God's love.
> *Hug.*

They believed that Jesus was God's Son. They were right!
> *Nod head yes.*

Every day Jesus and His disciples helped lots and lots of people. One day they were busy from the minute the sun came up.
> *Touch fingertips overhead to make the sun.*

Finally Jesus said, "Let's go across the lake and rest."
> *Wave good-bye.*

Jesus and the disciples got in a boat and set off across the lake.
> *Cup hands to make a boat sailing across the lake.*

Soon the stars began to twinkle in the sky.
> *Wiggle fingers to make twinkling stars.*

Jesus was so tired He lay down and fell asleep.

Rest cheek on hands.

The disciples talked softly as the boat sailed quietly on the water.

Hold finger to lips. "Shhhh."

Soon the wind began to blow.

Blow lightly.

Jesus was still asleep.

Rest cheek on hands.

Then it began to rain—just a little.

Snap fingers.

Then it rained harder and harder.

Quickly pat hands on legs.

The disciples pulled their robes over their heads to keep dry.

Cover head.

Jesus was still asleep.

Rest cheek on hands.

Then the lightning crackled and thunder boomed.

Loudly clap hands together.

Waves crashed into the sides of the boat.

Stamp feet, loudly clap hands, sway from side to side.

Jesus was still asleep!

Rest cheek on hands.

The disciples were afraid. They called out, "Jesus, save us!"

Cup hand around mouth.

Then Jesus woke up and said, "Stop!"

Hold up hand.

Suddenly the storm stopped. The wind was calm, and stars twinkled in the sky.

Wiggle fingers to make twinkling stars.

The disciples were amazed. Even the wind and waves listened to Jesus!

Clasp hand to cheek and gasp in amazement.

Dear Jesus, thank You for keeping me safe in storms and in any weather. You can do wonderful things. Amen.

✮ Remember the Story of Jesus Calming the Storm ✮

The next time it rains, stand with your child by a window or on the porch. If there is no lightning and it isn't too cool, go out and splash in the puddles. You can't make the rain stop or tell it where to land, but Jesus can. Say a thank-You prayer to God for the rain and the sun.

What's for Dinner?

Jesus Feeds the 5,000 *(Mark 6:30–44)*

Jesus and His disciples were tired.

Yawn.

Jesus said, "Let's go someplace quiet and rest."

Yawn and stretch.

Many people saw Jesus leave.

Cup hand over eyes.

They hurried and hurried to get to the quiet place where Jesus was going.

Quickly pat hands on legs.

When Jesus got to the quiet place, many people were there!

Clasp hand to cheek and gasp in amazement.

On this day many people came to see Jesus. There were more than 100.

Hold up one finger.

There were more than 500.

Hold up five fingers.

There were more than 1,000.

Hold up all 10 fingers.

On this day, there were more than 5,000 people who wanted to hear Jesus.

Spread arms wide.

Jesus loved the people. He was happy to talk to them.

Smile and place hands over heart.

Everyone listened to Jesus.

Point to ears.

Soon the sun started to set, and the disciples said to Jesus, "Send the people away to get their supper."

Point away from you.

But Jesus said to them, "You feed the people."

Point as if pointing to the disciples.

"That would take a lot of money!" the disciples said. "We can't do that."

Shake head no.

Jesus said, "Bring Me the food that you have."

Hold palms out in front.

One little boy had brought his lunch. He had two fish…

Hold up two fingers.

And five loaves of bread.

Hold up five fingers.

Not much food for all those people!

Hold palms out and shrug.

Jesus blessed the food and told the people to sit down.

Hold hands out as if in blessing.

Jesus told His disciples to feed the people. Will there be enough food?

Scratch head in confusion.

The disciples gave food to 100 people. There was still more!

Hold up one finger and nod head yes.

They gave food to 500 people. There was still more!

Hold up five fingers and nod head yes.

They gave food to 1,000 people. There was still more!

Hold up all 10 fingers and nod head yes.

Finally they gave food to all the people. Everyone had enough to eat!

Rub tummy.

Even after everyone was full, the disciples picked up 12 baskets of leftovers.

What do we do with leftovers?

The people thanked Jesus.

Fold hands.

Dear God, thank You for the bread and the fish we eat, and also bananas and peanut butter and ice cream. I know all good things come from You. In Jesus' name. Amen.

✵ Remember the Story of Jesus Feeding the 5,000 ✵

Plan a family picnic. If it's raining or cold, hold the picnic on the living room floor! Thank God for giving us good food to eat and for always taking such good care of us.

Dust and Sweep and Bake

Jesus Visits Mary and Martha *(Luke 10:38–42)*

Mary and her sister, Martha, lived in a little house in Bethany.
Touch fingertips together to make a house.
Mary and Martha had one very special friend.
Hold up one finger.
That friend's name was Jesus. Jesus taught Mary and Martha about God's love.
What do you know about Jesus?
One day Mary and Martha got wonderful news. Jesus was coming to visit them!
Clap hands. "Hooray!"
Martha cleaned and swept the floor and baked.
Pretend to sweep.
Mary gathered beautiful flowers for the table and watched for Jesus to come up the road.
Shade eyes and look far away.
Suddenly Mary called, "Jesus is here!"
Point to Jesus in the picture.
Jesus greeted Mary and Martha.
Hug.
Jesus sat down. Mary sat on the floor next to Him so she could

hear every word He said.

Pat the floor.

But Martha was too busy to sit down.

Shake head no.

Martha washed the special bowls and cups.

Pretend to wash dishes.

Martha took hot bread out of the oven.

Cup hands as if holding bread.

Martha set fruit and cheese on the table.

Pretend to set food on a table.

Martha opened the window so Jesus would feel the breeze.

Fan yourself.

Mary just sat.

Pat ground.

Mary sat and listened to Jesus.

Point to ears.

Martha said, "Jesus, tell Mary to help me."

Point to Mary and Martha in the picture.

Jesus said, "Martha, you have done such a good job of making Me feel welcome."

Nod head yes.

"What a nice house you have, and such good food."

Rub tummy.

"But now I have important news to tell you about God's love."

Hold hands over heart.

"Mary wants to hear My words."

Point to ears.

"Please sit with us."

Pat the floor.

"I want you to know about God's love too. God will love you always."

You can listen to Jesus and learn about God's love too!

Dear God, thank You for sending Your Son, Jesus, to be a friend to everyone. Help me to listen to Your Word. I want to know all about Your love! Amen.

✫ Remember the Story of Mary and Martha ✫

Plan the next day's schedule with your child. First schedule time around celebrating God's Word—set out a Bible story to read or place your family Bible on the kitchen table so you can look at it together during breakfast. Then plan some helping and playing activities for the rest of the day.

Come Sit with Jesus

Jesus Blesses the Children
(Mark 10:13–16)

One day mothers hurried to get their children ready. They washed their children's faces.

Rub face.

They gave the babies a bath and wrapped them in clean blankets.

Cradle arms to carry baby.

They did all this because Jesus was coming to town!

Clap hands. "Hooray!"

The mothers wanted Jesus to bless their babies and children.

What would you say to Jesus?

The disciples saw the mothers coming.

Shade eyes with hand.

They said, "Jesus is very busy teaching right now."

Shake finger no.

"He does not have time to spend with children."

Shake head no.

The mothers were so sad.

Make a sad face.

Jesus said, "Wait!"

Hold up hand in a "stop" gesture.

"Bring the children to Me. I want to see them and bless them."

Stretch out arms in a welcoming gesture.

"Everyone should love and believe in Me like these little children do."

Place hands over heart.

The mothers handed their babies to Jesus so He could bless them.

Cradle arms and rock baby.

Jesus took the children on His lap and told them that God loved them very much!

"God loves you very much too!"

Dear Jesus, I know You always have time for me. Thank You for making me Your special child. Amen.

✶ Remember the Story of Jesus Blessing the Children ✶

Schedule personal time with each of your children this week. Leave the house if necessary to avoid distractions. Even a walk around the block will be a special time and a blessing for you both.

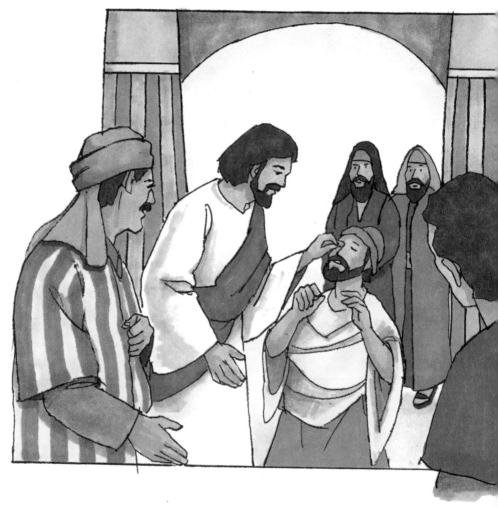

I Can See!

Jesus Heals Bartimaeus *(Mark 10:46–52)*

Bartimaeus was very sad.
>*Make a sad face.*

He could smell the flowers, but he could not see them.
>*Sniff.*

He could hear dogs, but he could not see them.
>*Bark like a dog.*

He could feel fuzzy caterpillars, but he could not see them.
>*Wiggle fingers up arm.*

Bartimaeus was blind. He could hear the donkey feet go *clip clop* on the road.
>*Pat hands on knees. "Clip, clop. Clip, clop."*

He could hear the birds singing in the trees.
>*Can you say "tweet-tweet" like the birds?*

He could hear people laughing.
>*Point to ears.*

More than anything, Bartimaeus wanted to see these things.
>*Point to eyes.*

One day Bartimaeus heard many people walking down the road.
>*Loudly pat hands on knees.*

Bartimaeus knew Jesus was coming!

Clap hands. "Hooray!"

Bartimaeus called loudly.

Call loudly, "Jesus, help me!"

The people said, "Don't bother Jesus!"

Hold finger to lips. "Shhhh!"

Bartimaeus called to Jesus at the top of his voice.

Shout loudly, "Jesus, help me!"

Then he waited and listened.

Did Jesus hear him?

Jesus said, "Bring Bartimaeus to me."

Hold arms out in welcoming gesture.

"Cheer up, Bartimaeus," the people said. "Jesus wants to meet you!"

Clap hands. "Hooray!"

Jesus said, "Bartimaeus, how can I help you?"

Hold hands out in questioning gesture.

Bartimaeus only wanted one thing. "I want to see," he said.

Close eyes and point to them.

Jesus touched Bartimaeus' eyes.

Put hands gently over eyes.

Slowly Bartimaeus opened his eyes.

Open eyes.

He could see the loving face of Jesus!

Clap hands. "Hooray!"

Maybe he could see a cat.

Can you purr?

Maybe he saw a butterfly.

Flutter your "wings."

Everywhere Bartimaeus looked, he saw wonderful things.

What do you like to see?

Bartimaeus joined the crowd of people following Jesus.

Pat hands on knees.

Everywhere he went he told others how Jesus helped him to see.

Point to eyes.

Bartimaeus was glad he met Jesus.

Smile.

Dear God, thank You for my eyes and everything that I see in Your wonderful world. I really like looking at all Your animals. In Jesus' name. Amen.

✷ Remember the Story of Bartimaeus ✷

Put familiar objects under a blanket or towel. Can your child guess what each object is by feeling the shape? Can smelling or listening help identify some objects? Together draw a picture of some of the favorite things your child sees outside and display it on the refrigerator.

Hosanna!

Jesus Rides into Jerusalem *(Matthew 21:1–16)*

Two disciples hurried down the road toward Jerusalem.

Hold up two fingers.

They were very excited and a little afraid.

How do you look when you're afraid?

"Do you think the little donkey will be where Jesus said?" one disciple asked.

Shrug.

"Well, Jesus stopped that storm the time we were on the water," said the other.

Hold up hand as if stopping the storm.

"And He fed all those people with just two fish and five loaves of bread."

Hold up five fingers on one hand and two on the other.

"If Jesus says we will find a donkey in the village, it will happen!"

Pound fist on hand and nod head yes.

They hurried toward Jerusalem.

Quickly pat hands on knees.

They found a donkey, just as Jesus had said.

"Hee-haw! Hee-haw!"

They led the little donkey to Jesus.

Lightly pat hands on knees. "Clip, clop. Clip, clop."
Jesus climbed on the back of the little donkey and rode it
toward Jerusalem. The little donkey walked quietly and did
not kick or bite at all.

Pat donkey's head. "Good donkey!"
Before long people heard Jesus was coming.
They ran out to see Him.

*Quickly pat hands on
knees.*

"Hosanna!" they
shouted. "Blessed is He
who comes in the name
of the Lord."

*Wave arms and
shout, "Hosanna!"*

They spread their coats on the ground to make a wonderful carpet for the little donkey to walk on.

Pretend to spread a piece of clothing on the ground.

The boys and girls pulled branches off the palm trees to wave at Jesus.

Wave a palm branch.

What an exciting parade!

Clap hands. "Hooray!"

Dear God, I like parades. I'm glad Jesus is my king. Hooray! Hosanna! Amen.

☆ Remember the Story of Palm Sunday ☆

Fold several sheets of paper in half and cut out large leaf shapes. Let your child color several leaves green. Then cut slits in the sides of the leaves so they can be waved like palm branches. Say together, "Hosanna! Blessed is He who comes in the name of the Lord!"

On the Cross

Jesus Dies for Us *(Mark 15:20–39)*

Jesus taught in the temple. Many people were glad to hear about God's kingdom.

Smile.

But some people did not like the idea of Jesus being a king.

Make a mean face.

They made secret plans to take Jesus from His friends.

Hold finger to lips with a stern look. "Shhhh!"

On Thursday night the disciples ate dinner with Jesus.

Rub tummy.

After supper they all went to the garden to pray.

Fold hands.

Jesus prayed.

Fold hands.

But the disciples fell asleep.

Rest head on hands.

Suddenly there was a loud noise!

Loudly pat hands on knees.

Soldiers came and took Jesus from His friends. The disciples were afraid!

Clap hands to cheeks in fear.

The disciples ran away. No one stayed with Jesus.

Shake head sadly.

The king said Jesus had to die.

Shake head sadly.

Soldiers led Jesus to a hill.

Slowly pat hands on knees.

A man helped Jesus carry a heavy cross.

How do you carry something that's very heavy?

The soldiers put Jesus on the cross. They set the cross up on the hill.

Make cross with two fingers.

Some people made faces at Jesus and laughed at Him.

Point and make a jeering face.

Jesus' friends were so sad to see Jesus hurt.

Cover face with hands and shake head sadly.

Jesus cried out loudly and died.

How do you think Jesus' friends felt?

A soldier said, "Jesus was the Son of God."

Nod head yes. "He was right."

Jesus died to take the punishment for the bad things we do.

Shake finger as if scolding.

But Jesus isn't mad at us.

Shake head no.

He was happy to die for us because He loves us.

Smile and place hands over heart.

....

Dear Jesus, it must have been a very sad day when You died. Thank You for loving me so much. Amen.

✸ Remember the Story of Jesus' Death ✸

Look around your home for crosses—pictures, crucifixes, necklaces. Look for crosses when you go to church. Remind your child that a cross helps us remember how much Jesus loves us.

Jesus Is Alive!

Jesus' Resurrection *(Matthew 27:57–58:15)*

Jesus' friends were very sad.
Shake head sadly.
Jesus had died on the cross.
Make a cross with two fingers.
His friends took Jesus' body to a garden and put it in a tomb that looked like a cave.
Touch index finger and thumb to palm to make a cave.
They rolled a big stone in front of the cave.
Circle hands around each other in a rolling motion.
One day passed.
Hold up one finger.
Two days passed.
Hold up two fingers.
Jesus' friends were so sad.
Shake head sadly.
Then the third day came.
Hold up three fingers.
It was very early.
Rub eyes sleepily.

Mary got up and got dressed.

Can you dress yourself?

She and her friends wanted to go to the cave to anoint Jesus' body. They took good-smelling lotion.

Sniff and smile.

The women walked quickly to the garden.

Softly pat hands on knees.

They said, "How will we move the big stone away?"

Circle hands around one another in a rolling motion.

When they came to the garden the sun was just coming up.

Touch fingertips overhead to make the sun.

Birds began to sing.

"Twitter-tweet!"

Guess what! The stone was rolled away!

Circle hands around each other in a rolling motion.

The women saw an angel!

Gasp in excitement.

The angel said, "Jesus is not here. He is alive!"

Clap hands. "Hooray!"

The women ran to tell Jesus' disciples.

Quickly pat hands on knees.

Suddenly they saw Jesus Himself!
Clap hands to face in joy.

Jesus said, "Tell My friends that I am alive, just as I said I would be."

Clap hands. "Hooray!"

Now the women weren't afraid.

Shake head no.

They were happy.

Smile.

They ran all the way back to Jerusalem.

Quickly pat hands on knees.

They found the disciples and said, "We have seen Jesus. He is alive!"

Say it with them, "Jesus is alive!"

....

Dear God, what happy news! Jesus is not dead anymore. He is alive. I will live with Him forever. Hooray! Amen.

✯ Remember Jesus' Resurrection ✯

Every morning brings a new chance to celebrate Jesus' resurrection. As you awaken your child repeat the words of the Easter women, "Jesus is alive!" What a wonderful way to start the day!

Breakfast Together

Jesus and the Disciples by the Sea of Galilee
(John 21:3–4, 12–17)

What an exciting week the disciples had!

Wipe brow. "Whew!"

First there was the big parade when Jesus rode the donkey.

Pat hands on knees. "Clip, clop. Clip, clop."

Then Jesus died on the cross.

Form cross with two fingers.

Jesus' friends put His body in a tomb.

Touch index finger and thumb to palm to form cave.

But Jesus rose again!

Clasp hands to cheeks in joy.

The disciples decided to go out in a boat and fish.

Can you row a boat like the disciples?

They saw someone far away on the shore.

Shade eyes to look far away.

It was Jesus!

How do you think the disciples felt when they saw Jesus?

Peter was so excited that he jumped into the water and swam to shore.

Make swimming motion. "Splash, splash, splash!"

Jesus and the disciples cooked fish for breakfast.

Rub hands together with pleasure. "Mmmmm."

Jesus asked, "Peter, do you love Me?"

Point to Jesus in the picture.

Peter said, "I do love You."

Point to Peter in the picture.

Jesus said, "Tell everyone about My love."

Clasp hands over heart.

How happy the disciples were. Their friend Jesus was with them again.

Hug self happily.

....

Dear Jesus, I'm so glad You are with me. I'm glad that I will live with You forever. Thank You! Amen.

✸ Remember the Story of Jesus' Special Breakfast ✸

Spread a picnic blanket on the grass or in the living room. Have a snack—maybe some fish-shaped crackers! Say a prayer of thanks for the food. Thank God for giving His Son's life for you and for taking such good care of you.

Peter said, "I do love You."

Point to Peter in the picture.

Jesus said, "Tell everyone about My love."

Clasp hands over heart.

How happy the disciples were. Their friend Jesus was with them again.

Hug self happily.

....

Dear Jesus, I'm so glad You are with me. I'm glad that I will live with You forever. Thank You! Amen.

✶ Remember the Story of Jesus' Special Breakfast ✶

Spread a picnic blanket on the grass or in the living room. Have a snack—maybe some fish-shaped crackers! Say a prayer of thanks for the food. Thank God for giving His Son's life for you and for taking such good care of you.